I0482343

MAINTENANCE LOG

Log Book Number ____________

Continued From Log Book Number ____________

Continued to Log Book Number ____________

Assigned To:

Name ____________

Signature ____________

Date ____________

Date Issued ____________

Issued By ____________

Phone ____________

Email ____________

Company ____________

Department ____________

Address ____________

Mail Stop ____________

City ____________

State ____________

ZIP ____________

Date Log Book Completed ____________

Number of Log Book Pages Completed ____________

Notes:

MAINTENANCE LOG BOOK

Log Book #____________

Date / Time	Maintenance / Comments	Signature

MAINTENANCE LOG BOOK

Log Book #____________

Date / Time	Maintenance / Comments	Signature

MAINTENANCE LOG BOOK

Log Book #____________

Date / Time	Maintenance / Comments	Signature

MAINTENANCE LOG BOOK

Log Book #_____________

Date / Time	Maintenance / Comments	Signature

MAINTENANCE LOG BOOK

Log Book #____________

Date / Time	Maintenance / Comments	Signature

MAINTENANCE LOG BOOK

Log Book #____________

Date / Time	Maintenance / Comments	Signature

MAINTENANCE LOG BOOK

Log Book #____________

Date / Time	Maintenance / Comments	Signature

MAINTENANCE LOG BOOK

Log Book #____________

Date / Time	Maintenance / Comments	Signature

MAINTENANCE LOG BOOK

Log Book #____________

Date / Time	Maintenance / Comments	Signature

MAINTENANCE LOG BOOK

Log Book #____________

Date / Time	Maintenance / Comments	Signature

MAINTENANCE LOG BOOK

Log Book #_____________

Date / Time	Maintenance / Comments	Signature

MAINTENANCE LOG BOOK

Log Book #____________

Date / Time	Maintenance / Comments	Signature

MAINTENANCE LOG BOOK

Log Book #______________

Date / Time	Maintenance / Comments	Signature

MAINTENANCE LOG BOOK

Log Book #_____________

Date / Time	Maintenance / Comments	Signature

MAINTENANCE LOG BOOK

Log Book #____________

Date / Time	Maintenance / Comments	Signature

MAINTENANCE LOG BOOK

Log Book #____________

Date / Time	Maintenance / Comments	Signature

MAINTENANCE LOG BOOK

Log Book #____________

Date / Time	Maintenance / Comments	Signature

MAINTENANCE LOG BOOK

Log Book #____________

Date / Time	Maintenance / Comments	Signature

MAINTENANCE LOG BOOK

Log Book #_______________

Date / Time	Maintenance / Comments	Signature

MAINTENANCE LOG BOOK

Log Book #_____________

Date / Time	Maintenance / Comments	Signature

MAINTENANCE LOG BOOK

Log Book #_____________

Date / Time	Maintenance / Comments	Signature

MAINTENANCE LOG BOOK

Log Book #______________

Date / Time	Maintenance / Comments	Signature

MAINTENANCE LOG BOOK

Log Book #____________

Date / Time	Maintenance / Comments	Signature

MAINTENANCE LOG BOOK

Log Book #____________

Date / Time	Maintenance / Comments	Signature

MAINTENANCE LOG BOOK

Log Book #______________

Date / Time	Maintenance / Comments	Signature

MAINTENANCE LOG BOOK

Log Book #____________

Date / Time	Maintenance / Comments	Signature

MAINTENANCE LOG BOOK

Log Book #____________

Date / Time	Maintenance / Comments	Signature

MAINTENANCE LOG BOOK

Log Book #____________

Date / Time	Maintenance / Comments	Signature

MAINTENANCE LOG BOOK

Log Book #____________

Date / Time	Maintenance / Comments	Signature

MAINTENANCE LOG BOOK

Log Book #____________

Date / Time	Maintenance / Comments	Signature

MAINTENANCE LOG BOOK

Log Book #______________

Date / Time	Maintenance / Comments	Signature

MAINTENANCE LOG BOOK

Log Book #____________

Date / Time	Maintenance / Comments	Signature

MAINTENANCE LOG BOOK

Log Book #______________

Date / Time	Maintenance / Comments	Signature

MAINTENANCE LOG BOOK

Log Book #____________

Date / Time	Maintenance / Comments	Signature

MAINTENANCE LOG BOOK

Log Book #____________

Date / Time	Maintenance / Comments	Signature

MAINTENANCE LOG BOOK

Log Book #____________

Date / Time	Maintenance / Comments	Signature

MAINTENANCE LOG BOOK

Log Book #____________

Date / Time	Maintenance / Comments	Signature

MAINTENANCE LOG BOOK

Log Book #_____________

Date / Time	Maintenance / Comments	Signature

MAINTENANCE LOG BOOK

Log Book #_____________

Date / Time	Maintenance / Comments	Signature

MAINTENANCE LOG BOOK

Log Book #_____________

Date / Time	Maintenance / Comments	Signature

MAINTENANCE LOG BOOK

Log Book #______________

Date / Time	Maintenance / Comments	Signature

MAINTENANCE LOG BOOK

Log Book #______________

Date / Time	Maintenance / Comments	Signature

MAINTENANCE LOG BOOK

Log Book #____________

Date / Time	Maintenance / Comments	Signature

MAINTENANCE LOG BOOK

Log Book #____________

Date / Time	Maintenance / Comments	Signature

MAINTENANCE LOG BOOK

Log Book #______________

Date / Time	Maintenance / Comments	Signature

MAINTENANCE LOG BOOK

Log Book #____________

Date / Time	Maintenance / Comments	Signature

MAINTENANCE LOG BOOK

Log Book #______________

Date / Time	Maintenance / Comments	Signature

MAINTENANCE LOG BOOK

Log Book #______________

Date / Time	Maintenance / Comments	Signature

MAINTENANCE LOG BOOK

Log Book #______________

Date / Time	Maintenance / Comments	Signature

MAINTENANCE LOG BOOK

Log Book #______________

Date / Time	Maintenance / Comments	Signature

MAINTENANCE LOG BOOK

Log Book #____________

Date / Time	Maintenance / Comments	Signature

MAINTENANCE LOG BOOK

Log Book #_____________

Date / Time	Maintenance / Comments	Signature

MAINTENANCE LOG BOOK

Log Book #______________

Date / Time	Maintenance / Comments	Signature

MAINTENANCE LOG BOOK

Log Book #______________

Date / Time	Maintenance / Comments	Signature

MAINTENANCE LOG BOOK

Log Book #____________

Date / Time	Maintenance / Comments	Signature

MAINTENANCE LOG BOOK

Log Book #______________

Date / Time	Maintenance / Comments	Signature

MAINTENANCE LOG BOOK

Log Book #______________

Date / Time	Maintenance / Comments	Signature

MAINTENANCE LOG BOOK

Log Book #______________

Date / Time	Maintenance / Comments	Signature

MAINTENANCE LOG BOOK

Log Book #____________

Date / Time	Maintenance / Comments	Signature

MAINTENANCE LOG BOOK

Log Book #______________

Date / Time	Maintenance / Comments	Signature

MAINTENANCE LOG BOOK

Log Book #______________

Date / Time	Maintenance / Comments	Signature

MAINTENANCE LOG BOOK

Log Book #_____________

Date / Time	Maintenance / Comments	Signature

MAINTENANCE LOG BOOK

Log Book #____________

Date / Time	Maintenance / Comments	Signature

MAINTENANCE LOG BOOK

Log Book #______________

Date / Time	Maintenance / Comments	Signature

MAINTENANCE LOG BOOK

Log Book #______________

Date / Time	Maintenance / Comments	Signature

MAINTENANCE LOG BOOK

Log Book #______________

Date / Time	Maintenance / Comments	Signature

MAINTENANCE LOG BOOK

Log Book #______________

Date / Time	Maintenance / Comments	Signature

MAINTENANCE LOG BOOK

Log Book #____________

Date / Time	Maintenance / Comments	Signature

MAINTENANCE LOG BOOK

Log Book #_______________

Date / Time	Maintenance / Comments	Signature

MAINTENANCE LOG BOOK

Log Book #_____________

Date / Time	Maintenance / Comments	Signature

MAINTENANCE LOG BOOK

Log Book #_____________

Date / Time	Maintenance / Comments	Signature

MAINTENANCE LOG BOOK

Log Book #______________

Date / Time	Maintenance / Comments	Signature

MAINTENANCE LOG BOOK

Log Book #______________

Date / Time	Maintenance / Comments	Signature

MAINTENANCE LOG BOOK

Log Book #_____________

Date / Time	Maintenance / Comments	Signature

MAINTENANCE LOG BOOK

Log Book #____________

Date / Time	Maintenance / Comments	Signature

MAINTENANCE LOG BOOK

Log Book #______________

Date / Time	Maintenance / Comments	Signature

MAINTENANCE LOG BOOK

Log Book #____________

Date / Time	Maintenance / Comments	Signature

MAINTENANCE LOG BOOK

Log Book #______________

Date / Time	Maintenance / Comments	Signature

MAINTENANCE LOG BOOK

Log Book #______________

Date / Time	Maintenance / Comments	Signature

MAINTENANCE LOG BOOK

Log Book #______________

Date / Time	Maintenance / Comments	Signature

MAINTENANCE LOG BOOK

Log Book #______________

Date / Time	Maintenance / Comments	Signature

MAINTENANCE LOG BOOK

Log Book #____________

Date / Time	Maintenance / Comments	Signature

MAINTENANCE LOG BOOK

Log Book #______________

Date / Time	Maintenance / Comments	Signature

MAINTENANCE LOG BOOK

Log Book #______________

Date / Time	Maintenance / Comments	Signature

MAINTENANCE LOG BOOK

Log Book #______________

Date / Time	Maintenance / Comments	Signature

MAINTENANCE LOG BOOK

Log Book #_____________

Date / Time	Maintenance / Comments	Signature

MAINTENANCE LOG BOOK

Log Book #______________

Date / Time	Maintenance / Comments	Signature

MAINTENANCE LOG BOOK

Log Book #____________

Date / Time	Maintenance / Comments	Signature

MAINTENANCE LOG BOOK

Log Book #______________

Date / Time	Maintenance / Comments	Signature

MAINTENANCE LOG BOOK

Log Book #_____________

Date / Time	Maintenance / Comments	Signature

MAINTENANCE LOG BOOK

Log Book #______________

Date / Time	Maintenance / Comments	Signature

MAINTENANCE LOG BOOK

Log Book #______________

Date / Time	Maintenance / Comments	Signature

MAINTENANCE LOG BOOK

Log Book #______________

Date / Time	Maintenance / Comments	Signature

MAINTENANCE LOG BOOK

Log Book #______________

Date / Time	Maintenance / Comments	Signature

MAINTENANCE LOG BOOK

Log Book #______________

Date / Time	Maintenance / Comments	Signature

MAINTENANCE LOG BOOK

Log Book #______________

Date / Time	Maintenance / Comments	Signature

MAINTENANCE LOG BOOK

Log Book #_____________

Date / Time	Maintenance / Comments	Signature

MAINTENANCE LOG BOOK

Log Book #______________

Date / Time	Maintenance / Comments	Signature

MAINTENANCE LOG BOOK

Log Book #______________

Date / Time	Maintenance / Comments	Signature

MAINTENANCE LOG BOOK

Log Book #______________

Date / Time	Maintenance / Comments	Signature

MAINTENANCE LOG BOOK

Log Book #______________

Date / Time	Maintenance / Comments	Signature

MAINTENANCE LOG BOOK

Log Book #______________

Date / Time	Maintenance / Comments	Signature

MAINTENANCE LOG BOOK

Log Book #______________

Date / Time	Maintenance / Comments	Signature

MAINTENANCE LOG BOOK

Log Book #______________

Date / Time	Maintenance / Comments	Signature

MAINTENANCE LOG BOOK

Log Book #______________

Date / Time	Maintenance / Comments	Signature

MAINTENANCE LOG BOOK

Log Book #____________

Date / Time	Maintenance / Comments	Signature

MAINTENANCE LOG BOOK

Log Book #______________

Date / Time	Maintenance / Comments	Signature

MAINTENANCE LOG BOOK

Log Book #______________

Date / Time	Maintenance / Comments	Signature

MAINTENANCE LOG BOOK

Log Book #____________

Date / Time	Maintenance / Comments	Signature

MAINTENANCE LOG BOOK

Log Book #_____________

Date / Time	Maintenance / Comments	Signature

www.ingramcontent.com/pod-product-compliance
Lightning Source LLC
Chambersburg PA
CBHW080705190526
45169CB00006B/2255
* 9 7 8 1 5 3 3 1 5 0 9 8 1 *